790.1 McI

PROJECTS FOR SUMMER & HOLIDAY
ACTIVITIES

McInnes, Celia

DEMCO

PROJECTS FOR SUMMER
& HOLIDAY ACTIVITIES

Celia McInnes

Illustrated by Stephen Wheele

 GARRETT EDUCATIONAL CORPORATION

Seasonal Projects
Projects for Spring & Holiday Activities
Projects for Summer & Holiday Activities
Projects for Autumn & Holiday Activities
Projects for Winter & Holiday Activities
Projects for Christmas
Projects for Easter

Text © 1989 by Garrett Educational Corporation

First published in the United States in 1989 by
Garrett Educational Corporation,
130 East 13th Street, Ada, OK 74820

First published in 1988 by
Wayland (Publishers) Limited, England
© 1988 Wayland (Publishers) Ltd, England

Library of Congress Cataloging-in-Publication Data

McInnes, Celia.
    Projects for summer & holiday activities.

    (Seasonal Projects)
    Includes index.
    Summary: Presents handicraft, recipes, games, activities, and informational articles relating to the summer season.
    1. Creative activities and seatwork — Juvenile literature.
2. Summer—Juvenile literature. [1. Handicraft. 2. Summer] I. Title.
II. Title: Projects for summer and holiday activities. III. Series.
GV1203.M3562   1989   790.1'922   89-11791

ISBN 0-944483-39-9

© Copyright 1989 Wayland (Publishers) Ltd

Typeset by Direct Image Photosetting Limited, Hove, East Sussex
Printed in Italy by Rotolito Lombarda, Milano
Bound in USA

Seasons do not happen at the same time of year all over the world. In the northern and southern halves of the world the seasons are reversed, as this chart shows:

Northern Hemisphere			
Spring	*Summer*	*Autumn*	*Winter*
March	June	September	December
April	July	October	January
May	August	November	February
Autumn	*Winter*	*Spring*	*Summer*
Southern Hemisphere			

Cover/left *Children playing in the park in summer.*

Cover/top right *Animal models.*

Cover/bottom right *Growing new plants from stem cuttings.*

Contents

Summer leaves   4
Leaf rubbing
Leaf stencil
Splatter print
The growing season   6
Potato maze
Colored flowers
Growth below ground   8
Leaf cuttings
Stem cuttings
Whitsuntide   10
Stick scrambler
Invisible writing
Well dressing   12
Flower mosaic
Using the sun   14
Sundial
Midsummer   16
Potpourri
Candied flower heads
At the seashore   18
Seaside scene
Shell box
In full flower   20
Flower press
Summer fruit   22
Summer fruit ice cream
Holidays and holy days   24
Corn dolly
Wildlife parks   26
Animal models
African festivals   28
Spirit mask

Glossary   30
Index   31

SUMMER LEAVES

An oak wood in June – the leaves of summer are a darker green than those of spring.

The leaves of summer are lush and dark compared with the delicate new growth of spring. In the countryside the tall grass is ready to be cut for hay, and in woods and parks the trees are green and shady.

Green leaves are the vital link between the sun's energy and life on earth. Plants and trees take in carbon dioxide through leaves, while the roots absorb water from the soil. The leaves use the carbon dioxide and water, and energy from sunlight, to make food in the form of sugars and starches. As they do so, they release oxygen into the air. This complex process is called photosynthesis, and is the basis for life on earth. Either directly or indirectly, plants provide food for animals and human life as well as producing the oxygen that we breathe.

Scientists believe the earth's atmosphere originally included little or no oxygen and that most of the oxygen it has now has been produced by green plants. This is why there is such concern over the destruction of the great rain forests of South America, Asia and Africa. These forests create oxygen for the whole world.

There is a huge variety of leaf shapes. Many can be used to make attractive patterns.

LEAF RUBBING

You will need:
- **a piece of paper that is fairly thin but strong**
- **wax crayons**
- **leaves with interesting rib patterns**

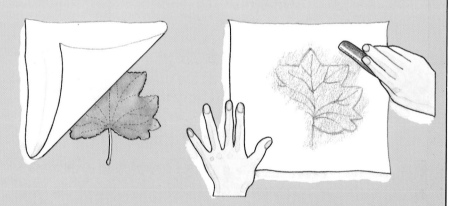

Lay the leaf face down on a flat surface and cover it with the paper. Hold the paper still and rub over the leaf with the flat part of the crayon, working from the center of the leaf outwards. Try a gold or silver crayon on dark paper.

LEAF STENCIL

You will need:
- a piece of paper
- poster paint
- a stiff brush
- a leaf

1 Lay the leaf on top of your piece of paper and hold it still while you apply fairly thick poster paint over its edges and onto the paper with a stiff brush. Dab with the brush, being careful not to go inside the line of the leaf edge.

2 Remove the leaf and you will have a stencil of its outline. Try white paint on colored paper.

SPLATTER PRINT

You will need:
- powder or poster paint
- a piece of paper
- a leaf
- a knife blade
- an old toothbrush (or similar brush)

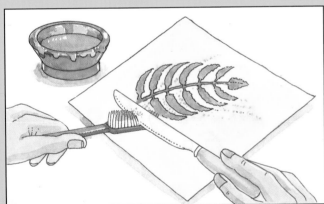

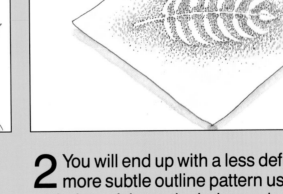

1 Mix some paint thickly and dip the bristles of the old toothbrush into it. Lay your leaf on the piece of paper and hold the brush over it at a slight angle. Run a knife blade over the bristles so that the paint splatters all over the paper and the leaf. Repeat.

2 You will end up with a less definite, more subtle outline pattern using this technique. It is particularly good with more delicate leaf shapes, such as those of ash and ferns. Experiment with more than one paint color and let the colors blend together.

THE GROWING SEASON

Summer is a good time to work with sprouting seeds and plants to find out how they grow. Two parts of a plant whose importance is not always recognized are the root and stem.

The root has two jobs: one is to hold the plant firmly in the ground. For example, a tall tree needs roots to take the strain as the wind blows it back and forth. The other job is to draw in water and minerals from the soil to feed the plant. Roots do this through tiny hairs.

In some plants food is stored in a thick taproot during the winter. In spring this food enables the leaves, flowers and seeds to develop. Examples of plants with taproots are carrots and turnips.

The stem contains veins that transport the water, minerals and food. It holds the plant upright or, in some species, it lies along the ground or clings to some support. The stem is a vital connection between the various parts of the plant, which are all working together to produce the seeds that will develop into new plants the next year.

When these young seeds leave the parent plant, they continue the same patterns of growth as the original stem and root. If the seed falls in a suitable

place, a shoot (stem) will break through the seed covering and grow up towards the light, and a root will grow down into the soil.

Stems and roots do this because they are responding to powerful natural forces: photo-tropism (growing towards the light) and geotropism (growing towards the ground). You can see phototropism in action every time

Above Summer is the season of growth for most plants, and the time when they produce flowers.

you turn a potted plant on a windowsill because it will lean towards the light. Cells in the plant stem on the side away from the light grow faster than those on the well-lit side, causing the stem to bend towards the light.

A POTATO MAZE

An amusing way of seeing phototropism at work is to make a potato maze.

You will need:
- a shoe box (or similar) with a lid
- a piece of cardboard
- a sprouting potato

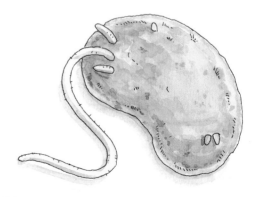

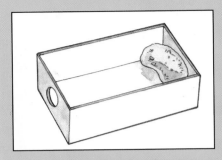

1 Place the potato at one end of the shoe box and cut a hole in the opposite end of the box.

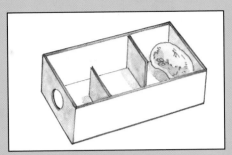

2 In between, fix two pieces of cardboard part way across the box. Attach one to the left-hand side, and one to the right-hand side, leaving gaps to make a maze.

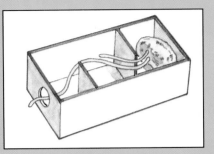

3 Put the lid on and place the box with the hole facing the light. The potato shoot will grow around the obstructions and eventually find its way out into the light. Take the lid off from time to time to check the shoot's progress.

COLORED FLOWERS

A dramatic way to demonstrate how stems work is to make colored flowers.

You will need:
- **a white flower, or a stalk of celery**
- **a jar of water**
- **colored ink**

1 Stand the flower, or celery, in water colored with ink.

2 Watch the flower change color as the ink is drawn up the stem. If you use celery, cut through it and you will see colored dots. These are the tubes through which the colored water passes up the stalk to the leaves.

GROWTH BELOW GROUND

Some plants do not show signs of growth above ground during the summer months. What happens instead is that their foliage dies back, perhaps disappearing completely, while growth continues below ground.

These plants have often grown from a bulb, corm or rhizome rather than a seed. A common example is the daffodil. Like most plants that grow from a bulb, the daffodil flowers in the spring. At the same time, the leaves make food, some of which is sent to the leaf bases. These swell and form a new bulb inside the old one. Food is also sent to one or more buds, called "lateral" buds, which are on the old bulbs. These grow to form daughter bulbs. The new bulb and daughter bulbs will produce a number of separate plants the following spring.

LEAF CUTTINGS

You too can grow new plants by making use of the food stored in leaves.

You will need:
- **an African violet plant**
- **a pot of moist potting soil**
- **a sharp knife**
- **a plastic bag**

1 Cut two or three leaves, with their stalks, off the plant.

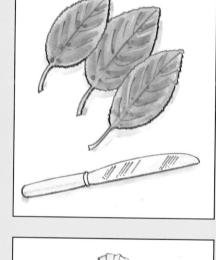

2 Put the leaf stalks into a pot of moist potting soil. Tie the plastic bag around the pot.

3 Leave the pot in a warm, light place, such as a windowsill, for a few weeks. Make sure the soil is kept moist.

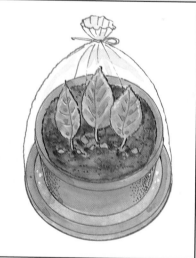

4 Tiny plants will appear where the leaf stalks go into the soil.

STEM CUTTINGS

You will need:
- a geranium plant
- a pot of moist potting soil
- rooting solution
- a sharp knife
- a plastic bag

1 Cut off a stem that is 3–6 in. long. Remove the lower leaves.

2 Cut the stem just below a point where a leaf was attached to it.

3 Dip the end of the stem into some rooting solution.

4 Plant the stem in the moist potting soil, pressing the soil firmly around the stem.

5 Tie the plastic bag around the pot and stem. The bag should not touch the leaves.

6 Keep the pot in a warm, light place and check that the potting soil stays moist.

7 After two to four weeks, when the cutting has developed roots, you can transfer it to a larger pot.

WHITSUNTIDE

Whitsuntide is one of the great festivals of the Christian Church and occurs in early summer. In the past there were many celebrations. A special drink was brewed, and the churches were decorated with greenery. In some places mystery plays, acting out Bible stories, were performed on wagons in the street.

Whitsun is the day the disciples of Jesus Christ received the Holy Spirit, giving them a feeling of peace and joy and the strength to go out and spread His teachings. The disciples had gathered in Jerusalem to celebrate Shavuot, the Jewish harvest festival that falls fifty days after Passover. In the same way, Whitsun is always fifty days after Easter (Pentecost, the Greek word for fifty, is applied to both festivals). Traditionally, many people were baptized at

A woman being baptized in a river in Jamaica.

Pentecost, which may be why its English name is Whitsun (White Sunday), after their white baptismal garments.

At the first Whitsun, the disciples received the "gift of tongues," which made it possible for them to be understood by all people. The disciple Peter immediately went out to preach to a large crowd gathered from many different countries. So we might say Whitsun is partly about communication.

STICK SCRAMBLER

There may be times when you want to communicate with someone secretly! This stick scrambler was first used thousands of years ago.

You will need:
- **2 sticks of the same diameter (pencils will do)**
- **a paper strip and sticky tape**

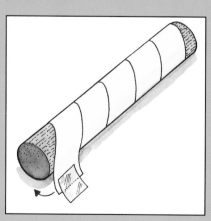

1 Wind the paper diagonally around and around the stick, along its length, and secure it in place with sticky tape.

2 Write the secret message along the stick, one letter on each wind of paper.

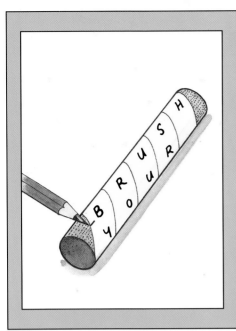

3 Put a small mark on the first "wind" to show where the message begins. More than one line should fit on the scrambler if you turn it around.

4 Remove the paper from the stick and you will see that your message is "scrambled"; only your contact can unscramble it by winding it around another stick of the same diameter.

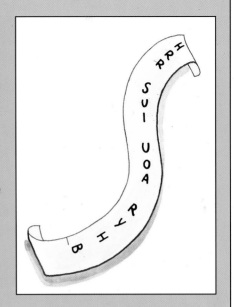

INVISIBLE WRITING

You can also use invisible writing to communicate in secret.

You will need:
- **a white candle**
- **sheets of paper**
- **a blunt pencil**

1 Rub plain white candle wax over one side of a sheet of paper.

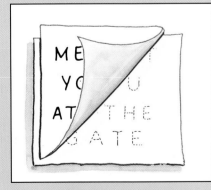

2 Lay the waxed side down on a piece of plain paper and write your message on the top sheet so that the marks go through to the sheet below.

3 Send the lower sheet to your contact, who can discover the message by powdering the page with, for example, chalk dust or cocoa powder.

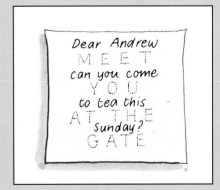

4 Rather than send a plain sheet, which might arouse suspicions, fit your wax writing between the lines of an ordinary "innocent" letter.

WELL DRESSING

The dressing of wells, such as this one in Derbyshire, England, is an ancient custom that still survives in some villages. It was adopted by the Christian Church and is now often associated with Ascensiontide.

Water is so important to human survival that many people have paid their respects to water spirits or believed rivers and wells to be magical or holy. The Jordan River and the Ganges River are believed to be holy. Beliefs in water gods were common in the Middle East. In ancient Rome, people threw flowers into wells to please the nymphs (water spirits), and in Britain Celtic people may even have made human sacrifices to their river gods. Today many people still throw money into wishing wells to bring themselves good luck, without even thinking about the significance of what they are doing.

The custom of decorating wells began in parts of England long before Christianity became an accepted religion. The Celts, for example, decorated wells with flowers to stop them from drying up over the summer. As with so many pagan customs, the Christian Church adopted this ritual to suit its own festivals. Many wells were given the names of saints and were used for baptism. In some areas the ancient custom of decorating the wells survived, often associated with Ascensiontide. This is the time in May or June (depending on the timing of Easter) when Christians remember how Christ's spirit went up to Heaven forty days after His crucifixion.

For well dressing, Biblical scenes and texts are marked out in clay spread over a wooden frame. The clay is then studded with natural decorations such as flower petals, buds, leaves, berries, moss, pine cones and feathers. This produces a glowing mosaic that is placed on the well to decorate it. You could make your own version, copying a picture from a book or following your own design.

A FLOWER MOSAIC

You will need:
- a shallow tray
- pottery clay
- a sharp pointed blade
- flower petals, leaves, buds, seeds, etc.
- a piece of drawing paper

1 Press a ½-in. layer of clay into the tray. It should be damp enough to keep the plant material fresh for as long as possible, but firm enough to hold it in place.

2 Plan your design on paper and then copy it on the clay, using a sharp pointed blade.

3 Fill in the outlines with whatever natural materials you can find to give the color and texture you need.
Try to get each piece of the mosaic in place the first time.

USING THE SUN

Without the sun there would be no life on earth. All living things need its light, warmth and energy to survive. However, it is fortunate that we are protected from its full power, for the sun is in fact a fiery star so hot that it could burn up our planet. Even though we are protected by being many millions of miles from the sun, we still need to be shielded from its rays. The earth's atmosphere protects us, letting only a portion of the sun's light and heat through. The ozone layer filters out most of the harmful ultraviolet rays. However, it now seems that we are damaging the ozone layer by releasing harmful chemicals into it. Unless we stop this, the sun's rays could alter our climate and damage us.

Every day the earth rotates completely around its axis. Because of this, the position of the sun in the sky appears to change, rising in the morning sky in the east and setting in the west in the evening. As a result, the length and the direction of shadows change throughout the day. By watching the changes in a shadow, you can get an approximate idea of the time – a fact on which sundials are based. Before the invention of clocks, sundials were the only way you could tell the time.

Can you tell from the sundial what time of day this photograph was taken?

A SUNDIAL

You can make a sundial from a block of wood and a simple leg. It will not give you the exact clock time but sun time, the natural time that animals live by.

You will need:
- **a piece of wood, about 10 in. square**
- **a compass and pencil**
- **pens or paints**
- **wooden doweling, about 6 in. long**
- **a hand drill**

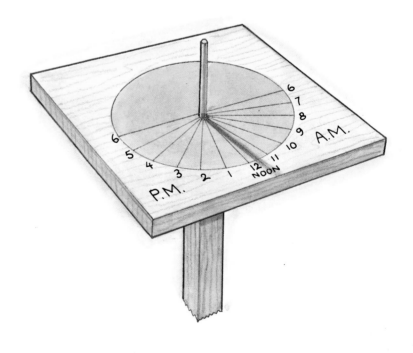

1 Set the compass to 4 in. and draw a circle on the wood. Divide one-half of this circle into twelve equal sections, ruling lines out from the center. (Use the top half of the circle for the Northern Hemisphere, the bottom half for the Southern.)

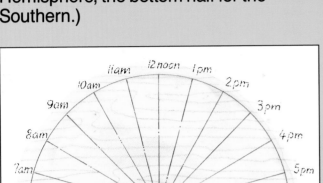

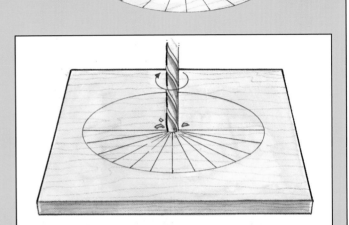

2 Pencil the daylight hours around this half-circle, starting with 6 am on the left and ending with 6 pm on the right.

3 Drill a hole at the center of the circle to hold the doweling in place, tightly upright.

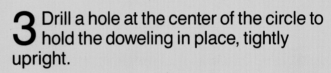

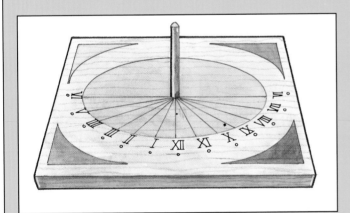

4 Paint or color over your pencil markings and decorate the whole sundial as you like. It can be quite plain, have bold Roman numerals, or be a riot of colorful patterns. Finish by varnishing if you like.

5 Place the sundial where it will catch the sunlight, so that the midday (12 o'clock) mark points north in the Northern Hemisphere, or south in the Southern Hemisphere. (When the sun's shadow is shortest, it points exactly north in the Northern Hemisphere, or south in the Southern Hemisphere.)

MIDSUMMER

At midsummer the sun is at its highest point in the sky and we experience the longest day – the day of the year with the most hours of daylight. For thousands of years this has been a time for celebration. In the past it was also a time for offering encouragement and sacrifices to the sun to help it maintain its vital strength.

The Incas in Peru used to hold a festival called Inti Raymi, the feast of the sun, to honor the sun at high summer. The Aztecs in Mexico offered up the most precious gift: human life. They believed that sacrificing people to the sun would enable it to continue rising every day. Many of the Plains Indians of North America performed a ceremonial sun dance as the highlight of their annual gatherings at midsummer. In Britain the summer solstice was honored with ceremonies at temples such as that at Stonehenge.

In much of Europe, June 21 was the occasion for huge bonfires, intended to boost the sun's power. In places tar barrels were lit, representing the sun at its zenith, or cartwheels were set on fire and rolled downhill, just as the sun would now follow its downward path in the sky. Evil spirits were believed to be about and the bonfires served to keep these away. So, too, did the flowers and herbs thrown on the fire. Afterwards the ashes might be kept as a charm or sprinkled on the fields for good luck. Young people also jumped over the fire for good luck. As Christianity spread, these customs were transferred to June 24, the feast of St. John.

Few people today mark the longest day in any special way, but they still enjoy the light, warm evenings of June. You could keep a memory of those days with a potpourri of June roses or with candied flowers.

POTPOURRI

You will need:
- 1 quart freshly gathered scented rose petals
- 1 tsp powdered cinnamon
- 1 cup mixture of sweet-smelling herbs and flowers (such as rosemary, lemon verbena, mock orange, lavender, rose, geranium)
- 1 heaping tsp dried orange or lemon peel, powdered
- 4–6 bay leaves
- 1 tsp powdered cloves
- 2 tbsp uniodized kitchen salt

1 To make the potpourri mix, spread the flowers and leaves out to dry somewhere warm but out of direct light.

2 When the petals, etc. are dry, mix all the ingredients (except salt) gently with the fingertips.

3 Put the potpourri mix into an airtight container, sprinkling it with a little salt after every ¾-in. layer.

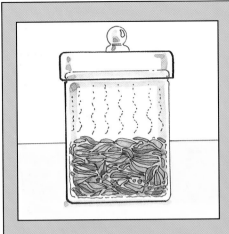

4 Leave for about a month for the fragrance to "set."

5 Sew the potpourri mix into sachets to keep in drawers and cupboards, or display in an open bowl to perfume a room.

CANDIED FLOWER HEADS

These make lovely decorations for summer cakes and special ice cream.

You will need:
- **any edible flower heads, e.g., rosebuds, primroses, violets, or apple, pear, plum or cherry blossoms**
- **white of an egg**
- **granulated sugar**
- **a fine paintbrush**

1 Pick your flowers when they are dry. Take care not to bruise the petals.

2 Holding each flower as gently as possible, paint all over, top and bottom, with the paintbrush dipped in egg white.

3 While the flower is still sticky, sprinkle granulated sugar over it to coat it thinly but completely.

4 Allow the flowers to dry. Store them in an airtight container.

AT THE SEASHORE

Summer vacations by the sea can provide many opportunities to explore the seashore. Here there are many plants and animals whose existence depends on the twice-daily rise and fall of the tide.

Tides are caused by the gravitational pull of the sun and moon. When the sun and moon are at right angles to each other, they pull against each other. The result is a very small tide, called a "neap" tide. When the sun and moon are lined up together, they exert a particularly large pull, which results in a "spring" tide. This rises and falls more than twice the distance of a neap tide and occurs about once every two weeks.

Different parts of the shore are uncovered for different lengths of time, so the plants and animals vary from one part to the next. For example, near the high-water mark there are types of seaweed that will survive being dried out up to 90 percent of the time. However, near the low-water mark there are seaweeds that can only tolerate being uncovered about 50 percent of the time.

A rocky seashore is the most interesting type to explore. Between and under the clumps of seaweed can be found mollusks, fish, crabs, starfish, sponges, sea anemones, sea urchins and worms.

You can find a huge variety of plants and animals at the seashore, particularly if it is rocky.

SEASIDE SCENE

You can make your own miniature seaside scene using seaweed and other objects collected from the beach.

You will need:
- **a sheet of cardboard**
- **paste and brush**
- **glue**
- **sand**
- **dried seaweed**
- **pebbles and shells**

1 Brush the paste evenly over one side of the cardboard and cover it with sand. Wait for the paste to dry and shake off any loose sand.

2 Arrange your pebbles, shells and pieces of seaweed on the sand and glue them in place.

SHELL BOX

You will need:
- **a small, strong cardboard box**
- **sealing wax**
- **glue**
- **colored paper**

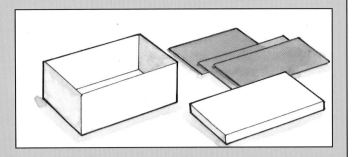

1 Cut out pieces of paper to cover the sides and bottom of the box. Stick them to the box with glue.

2 On a piece of paper, draw a rectangle that is exactly the same size as the top of your box. Arrange some shells on it in a pattern that you like.

3 Melt a little sealing wax over one section of the box top.

4 While the wax is soft, take the shells from the same section of your pattern and carefully place them in the wax.

5 Repeat steps 3 and 4 until the box top is covered by your pattern.

IN FULL FLOWER

Summer is the season of flowers, as parks, gardens and fields burst into color. But what are flowers for, and why do insects and other creatures like them so much?

The job of the flower is to produce seeds for the next generation of plants. Each flower is made up of outer sepals and petals, which protect the stamens and carpels – the parts that produce the seeds. Pollen from the stamens must be transferred to the sticky tips of the carpels (called "stigmas") if fertilization is to occur. Fertilization is the process by which seeds are formed. Most plants require pollen from another plant of the same kind for this to happen.

The bright colors and sweet scents of flowers help to attract insects, such as bees and butterflies. Insects are attracted because flowers contain a sugary food called nectar. They carry away grains of pollen on their bodies. As they move from flower to flower, pollen rubs off onto the stigmas of other flowers of the same kind, thereby pollinating (and fertilizing) them. This is known as cross-pollination.

Different flowers attract different pollinators. Most are insects, but fruit bats, hummingbirds and the honey possum are three other creatures that aid flower pollination by feeding on nectar. Among the insects, moths

Above The bright colors of flowers attract insects, such as bees. The insects act as pollinators, carrying grains of pollen from one flower to another.

are also important. They feed at night and so are attracted by pale flowers, which show up in the dark, or those that open only at night, such as the evening primrose. They are also attracted to the perfume of night-scented flowers such as nicotiana and honeysuckle.

One way to preserve flowers is to dry them and press them in a flower press. You can make your own flower press quite easily.

FLOWER PRESS

To preserve flowers, whether for study or for pleasure, a flower press is essential.

You will need:
- 2 pieces of plywood, about 8 in. square
- 6 pieces of corrugated cardboard, about 8 in. square
- 6 pieces of white blotting paper, about 8 in. square
- 4 wing nuts and bolts, about 3 in. long
- a hand drill

1 Drill a hole in each corner of one plywood square, large enough to allow a bolt to pass through.

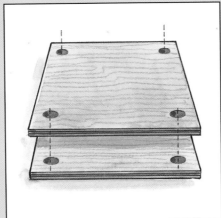

2 Lay this square on top of the other plywood square and drill through the top holes so that you have two matching sets of holes.

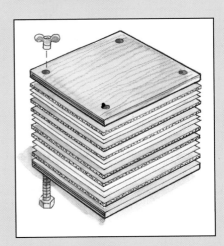

3 Arrange the cardboard and blotting paper in three "sandwiches." Each sandwich will be of cardboard, blotting paper (×2) and cardboard again.

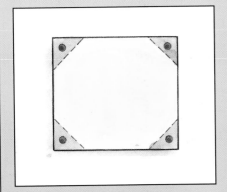

4 Trim the cardboard and paper corners so that the bolts do not have to pass through them.

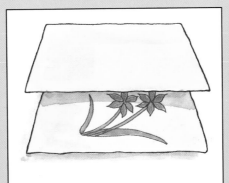

5 Carefully place the flowers that you want to press between the blotting paper layers of each sandwich.

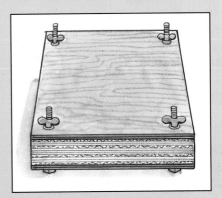

6 Insert the four bolts and tighten the wing nuts to put as much pressure as possible on the flowers inside.

SUMMER FRUIT

Fruits are produced by plants to carry their seeds. They include the fruits we enjoy eating.

When we look forward to summer fruit we usually think of such things as strawberries, cherries or peaches. But these are just the fruits that we have chosen to cultivate over the centuries. It is believed that fruit orchards were planted by the ancient Egyptians. Certainly, figs and grapes were cultivated in Rome 2,000 years ago.

The word "fruit," however, also covers cultivated foods that we think of as vegetables: a peapod is a fruit containing a number of seeds (the peas); so, too, is a cucumber. So what is a fruit?

A fruit is produced by a plant to help in the process of dispersing its seeds. It is important that the seeds are taken away from the parent plant. If they are not, they will compete with the parent plant for water and minerals in the soil, and for space in which to grow.

Almost all plants produce fruit: rose hips, holly berries, acorns and nuts all contain seeds and are all fruits. In many cases the fruit is eaten by a bird or animal. The seed may then be dropped a long distance away. This is why many fruits have juicy flesh and a sweet smell – to attract "carriers."

Some fruits, such as sycamore spinners and thistle parachutes, are spread by being blown away by the wind. Others, such as the tiny fruits of buttercups and sticky goosegrass, catch on animal fur and are dispersed that way. Some are carried away by water: coconuts have been known to germinate after floating across wide distances of open sea. Other fruits do not leave the parent plant. Poppy heads, for example, shake their seeds out onto the ground nearby.

SUMMER FRUIT ICE CREAM

You can choose a mixture of summer fruits to make your own special ice cream.

For two helpings you will need:
- ½ lb fruit such as apricots, strawberries peaches, pineapples or raspberries
- ½ tbsp very hot water in a cup
- ½ tsp gelatin
- 2 oz granulated sugar
- 6 tbsp heavy whipped cream
- a sieve
- a wooden spoon
- a mixing bowl
- a small ice tray

1 Use the wooden spoon to mash the fruit and put it through the sieve.

2 Sprinkle the gelatin into the hot water and stir briskly. The gelatin should dissolve quickly.

3 Mix the fruit, sugar and gelatin together in the bowl.

4 When the mixture is cold, beat it well and fold in the whipped cream.

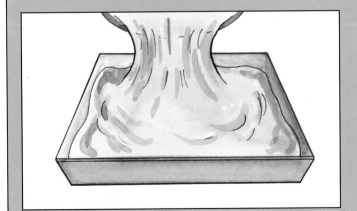

5 Pour the mixture into the ice tray and leave it in the freezer for three hours.

6 You can decorate the ice cream with candied flower heads (see page 17).

HOLIDAYS AND HOLY DAYS

Summer is the season in which people usually take their main vacation of the year. It is also the season in which many countries have national one-day holidays when the majority of people do not work. One of the best-known of these is Independence Day in the United States. Every year on July 4 all fifty-one states celebrate the adoption in 1776 of the Declaration of Independence by the original thirteen British colonies in North America.

In Canada, July 1 is a national holiday known as Canada Day. Canadians celebrate the union of the first four provinces as the Dominion of Canada in 1867.

Some national holidays have grown out of the "holy days" when, in the past, people stopped work to celebrate a festival. This would be their only opportunity for fun, as they had no free weekends and no paid time off.

One example of such a holy day during the summer months is Lammas, which was traditionally celebrated in England on August 1. Bread made from the first sheaf of wheat to be harvested was taken to the church to be blessed (hence, Loaf-mass, later blurred into Lammas). Nowadays, the August holiday is taken on the last Monday of the month and few people remember Lammas.

Independence Day in the United States is one of the best-known national one-day holidays. In Washington, D.C., it is celebrated with fireworks.

CORN DOLLY

In England a custom long associated with the harvesting of grain, or corn as it is called in England, is the making of corn dollies. They were once made from the last sheaf of grain to be harvested, in order to ensure a good harvest the following year. Nowadays, they are made just for decoration.

Corn dollies are traditionally made with five-straw braids that form a spiral shape. They may either be hollow or have a solid core made from a number of straws. You can use the following simplified method to make a hollow dolly.

You will need:
- 5 long straws of wheat or rye with ears
- several long straws without ears
- strong thread
- scissors
- ribbon

1 Soak all the straws for several hours in cold water until they are soft and easy to bend.

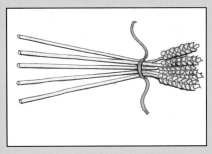

2 Use the thread to tie together the five straws with ears. Tie them just below the ears.

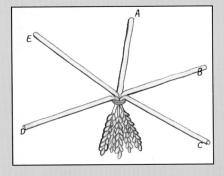

3 Bend the straws out so that they are horizontal.

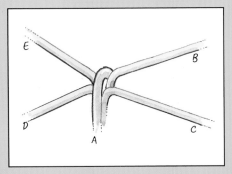

4 Take straw A and bend it towards you over the next two straws, B and C.

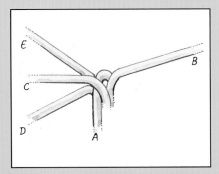

5 Take the second of these straws, C, and bend it over the next two straws, A and D.

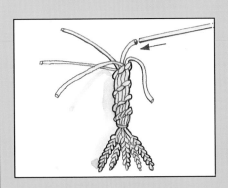

6 When you reach the end of a straw, insert a new one (without an ear) inside it, and continue as before.

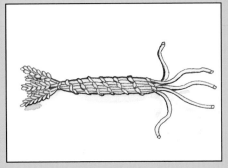

7 Try to make your dolly wider in the middle than at the end by braiding the straws more loosely.

8 Braid the last 2–4 in. as tightly as possible. Tie the end with strong thread and fold it back to form a loop. Decorate with a ribbon.

WILDLIFE PARKS

A warm summer's day is the best time for an outdoor outing to a wildlife or safari park, where animals can be seen living in natural surroundings. They include some of the largest in the world: the moose and buffalo from North America; the tiger from India and other countries in southern Asia; the elephant from India and Africa; the giraffe, rhinoceros, hippopotamus and gorilla from Africa. The African elephant is the largest animal of all, weighing over 15,000 lbs. It spends about eighteen hours a day feeding on grass, leaves and bark in order to maintain its vast size. Tallest of all is the giraffe. It is about 5 ft. tall at birth and can grow to about 18 ft.

Other animals to be found in a wildlife or safari park include members of the cat family, such as lions, leopards, cheetahs and pumas; monkeys and chimpanzees; and hoofed animals, such as deer, antelopes and zebras.

ANIMAL MODELS

For each animal you will need:
- **a toilet roll tube**
- **cardboard (about same thickness as tube)**
- **four cocktail sticks**
- **a large needle**
- **a thimble**
- **scissors**
- **glue**
- **Scotch tape**
- **poster paints**

You can make models of many animals found in a wildlife park, using the basic method described below.

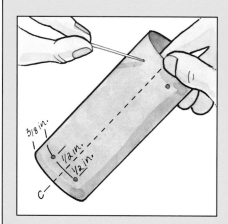

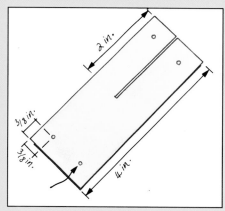

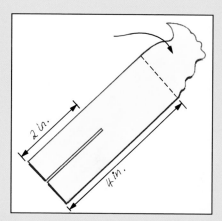

1 Use the needle and thimble to make two pinholes at each end of the tube. They should be about ³⁄₈ in. from the edge and 1 in. apart.

2 Cut a rectangle from the cardboard that is the same length as the tube and as wide as the diameter of the tube. Cut a slot that is half the length of the rectangle. Its width should be the same as the thickness of the cardboard. Make four pinholes ³⁄₈ in. in from the edges, as shown.

3 Cut a second piece of cardboard that is a rectangle (the same size as the first rectangle) with an extra piece on the end. Cut this extra piece in the shape of the animal's head. Cut a slot at the other end that is the same length and width as the slot in the first rectangle.

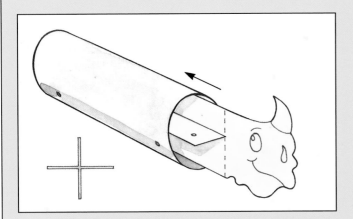

4 Slot the two rectangles together. Slide them into the tube, making sure the head is between the pinholes in the tube.

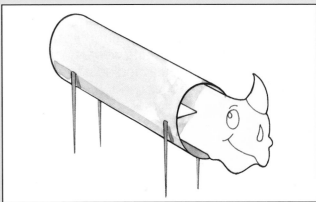

5 Push the cocktail sticks through the pinholes in the tube and in the horizontal rectangle.

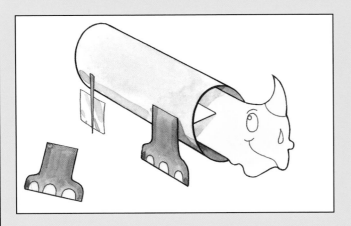

6 Cut out leg shapes and use Scotch tape to attach them to the cocktail sticks.

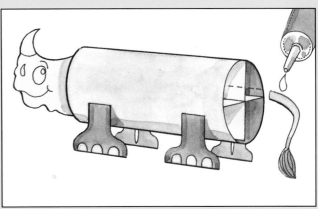

7 Cut out a tail and glue it to the vertical piece of cardboard.

8 Paint the animal with poster paints.

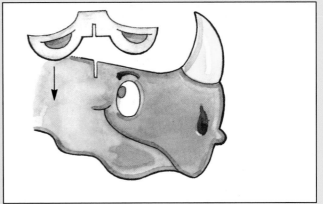

9 You can add horns or ears using the slotting method.

AFRICAN FESTIVALS

Africa is such a large continent that there is an enormous variety in the way people live. One end-of-summer festival that combines elements shared by many African countries is the celebration of the yam harvest in Ghana, West Africa. Yams (sweet potatoes) are the main food crop, so the harvest is an important occasion.

By the end of August, in Ghana's rainy season, the old yams have all been eaten, and everyone eagerly awaits the new crop. Even when the yams are harvested, however, nobody is allowed to eat them or even bring them into the markets or villages. This is because some yams have first to be ceremonially offered up to the god of the harvest and to the people's ancestors. Ancestors are honored because it is believed they have great influence.

After the priest has carried out these rituals, everyone eats a meal of new yams, then joins in parades and parties, with singing, dancing, playing of drums and the drinking of palm wine. It is an important day in the life of the community.

In Nigeria, another West African country, the yam is also an important crop. Similar harvest thanksgivings take place there. The Yoruba people of Nigeria are also known for their traditional festival of ancestor worship. They make offerings to the shrines of their ancestors' spirits, and dress up in elaborate costumes and masks, impersonating these spirits as they dance through the streets.

The Yoruba people of Nigeria wear masks during their festival of ancestor worship.

A SPIRIT MASK

To make a spirit mask you will need:
- **a balloon**
- **newspaper strips**
- **wallpaper paste**
- **raffia/straw**
- **elastic cord**
- **paints**

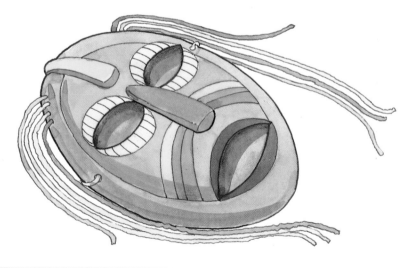

1 Blow up the balloon until it is about the size of your head. Knot the end.

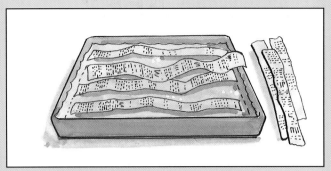

2 Soak the newspaper strips in wallpaper paste until soggy.

3 Wedge the balloon between two objects to hold it steady. Then paste newspaper strips over the front half. Make five layers like this.

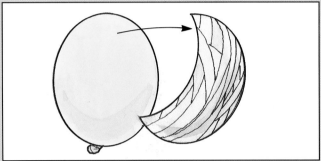

4 Leave to dry, then ease the papier-mâché shape off the balloon. Break the balloon if necessary. The papier-mâché should be firm and quite strong.

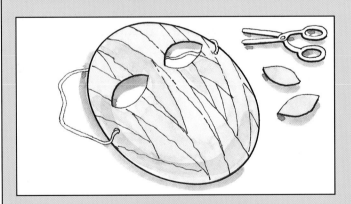

5 Cut eyeholes in the "head" and pierce holes at the sides to thread elastic through. Knot the elastic.

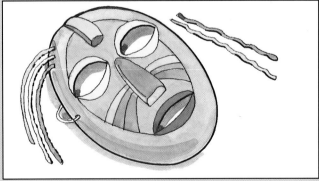

6 Paint the mask using thick poster paints. Give your mask a strong mouth and face decorations. Glue on straw raffia, or tissue paper, as "hair." If a local museum has any tribal masks, you could get some ideas from them.

Glossary

Aztecs The most famous of the tribes living in Mexico when it was conquered by the Spanish in the sixteenth century. Their cities were destroyed and their old ways and religion were stamped out by their Spanish conquerors.

Bulb An underground bud that consists of a short, thickened stem surrounded by a number of overlapping leaves. Contains food for the plant that will grow the following year.

Carpel The female part of a plant that grows into fruit and in which seeds develop.

Celts An ancient people who were predominant in central and western Europe before the influx of Germanic tribes and the rise of the Roman Empire. They had druids, or priests, who performed magical ceremonies.

Corm An underground stem base that is swollen with food. The plant that will grow the following year is surrounded by papery leaves.

Fertilization In a plant, the uniting of pollen and female cells to form a seed.

Ganges River The most sacred river of the Hindus. Flows from the Himalayas through north India and Bangladesh to the Bay of Bengal.

Geotropism A plant's response to the pull of gravity, which causes the roots to grow downwards.

Germination The early stage of a plant's growth when the seed begins to grow.

Incas A tribe of Indians who lived in Peru and founded the greatest civilization of ancient America. This civilization was destroyed by the Spanish in the sixteenth century.

Jordan River The chief river of Israel and Jordan. Flows through the sea of Galilee to the Dead Sea.

Mystery play A type of play, originally performed in the Middle Ages, which was based on the life of Christ.

Nectar A sweet, sugary liquid made inside a flower. It attracts insects that will help in the process of pollination.

Pentecost A Jewish feast held fifty days after Passover; from the Greek word for fifty.

Photosynthesis The complex process by which plants use carbon dioxide, water, and energy from sunlight to make their food.

Phototropism The growing of plant stems towards the light.

Pollination The transferring of pollen in flowers from anthers to carpels.

Rhizome A thick, underground horizontal stem. It has buds that develop into new plants.

Shavuot The Jewish harvest festival; falls fifty days after Passover.

Stamen The male part of a flower. Consists of a stalk and anther, which produces pollen.

Stonehenge An impressive prehistoric monument in southern England that was built approximately between 2500 and 1500 B.C. It had a religious meaning possibly associated with sun-worship, and may also have had something to do with astronomy (the study of the stars).

Tuber An underground stem or root from which new plants grow. It is also used to store food.

Yoruba A people who live mainly in the coastal regions of southwest Nigeria.

Picture acknowledgments

Oxford Scientific Films 4 (Terry Heathcote), 20 (G.A. Maclean), 22 (Michael Brooke); Paul Seheult (cover/bottom right); Ronald Sheridan 28; Topham 12, 14; Wayland 10 (John Wright); Tim Woodcock (cover/left); ZEFA 6, 18, 24.

Index

Africa **26**
Ancestor worship **4, 28**
Ancient Egyptians **22**
Ascensiontide **12**
Asia **4, 26**
Aztecs **16**

Britain **12, 16, 24**
Bulbs **8,**

Canada **24**
Canada Day **24**
Carpels **20**
Celts **12**
Corms **8**
Cross-pollination **20**

Feast of St. John **16**
Fertilization **20**
Fruits **22**

Geotropism **6**
Ghana **28**

Incas **16**

Lammas **28**

Midsummer Day **16**
Mystery plays **10**

Nigeria **28**
North America **16, 24, 26**

Oxygen **4**
Ozone layer **14**

Passover **10**
Pentecost **10**
Photosynthesis **4**
Phototropism **6**
Pollination **20**
Projects
    Animal models **26**
    Candied flower heads **17**
    Colored flowers **7**
    Corn dolly **24**
    Flower mosaic **13**
    Flower press **21**
    Invisible writing **11**
    Leaf cuttings **8**
    Leaf rubbing **4**
    Leaf stencil **5**
    Potpourri **16**
    Potato maze **6**
    Seaside scene **18**
    Shell box **19**
    Spirit mask **29**
    Splatter print **5**
    Stem cuttings **9**
    Stick scrambler **10**
    Summer fruit ice cream **22**
    Sundial **14**

Rhizomes **8**
Roots **6**

Seaweed **18**
Sepals **20**
Shavuot **10**
South America **4**
Stamens **20**
Stems **6**

Stonehenge **16**
Sundials **14**

Tides **18**

United States **24**

Well dressing **12**
Whitsun **10**

Yoruba people **28**